I USE MATH/USO LAS MATEMÁTICAS

I USE MATH AT THE DOCTOR'S/
USO LAS MATEMÁTICAS EN EL MÉDICO

Joanne Mattern

Reading consultant/Consultora de lectura: Susan Nations, M.Ed., author/literacy coach/consultant

WR WEEKLY READER
EARLY LEARNING LIBRARY

Please visit our web site at: www.earlyliteracy.cc
For a free color catalog describing Weekly Reader® Early Learning Library's list
of high-quality books, call 1-877-445-5824 (USA) or 1-800-387-3178 (Canada).
Weekly Reader® Early Learning Library's fax: (414) 336-0164.

Library of Congress Cataloging-in-Publication Data available upon request from publisher.
Fax (414) 336-0157 for the attention of the Publishing Records Department.

ISBN 0-8368-5999-5 (lib. bdg.)
ISBN 0-8368-6006-3 (softcover)

This edition first published in 2006 by
Weekly Reader® Early Learning Library
A Member of the WRC Media Family of Companies
330 West Olive Street, Suite 100
Milwaukee, WI 53212 USA

Managing editor: Valerie J. Weber
Art direction: Tammy West
Cover design and page layout: Dave Kowalski
Photo research: Diane Laska-Swanke
Photographer: Gregg Andersen
Translators: Tatiana Acosta and Guillermo Gutiérrez

Printed in the United States of America

1 2 3 4 5 6 7 8 9 09 08 07 06 05

Note to Educators and Parents

Reading is such an exciting adventure for young children! They are beginning to integrate their oral language skills with written language. To encourage children along the path to early literacy, books must be colorful, engaging, and interesting; they should invite the young reader to explore both the print and the pictures.

I Use Math is a new series designed to help children read about using math in their everyday lives. In each book, young readers will explore a different activity and solve math problems along the way.

Each book is specially designed to support the young reader in the reading process. The familiar topics are appealing to young children and invite them to read and reread again and again. The full-color photographs and enhanced text further support the student during the reading process.

In addition to serving as wonderful picture books in schools, libraries, homes, and other places where children learn to love reading, these books are specifically intended to be read within an instructional guided reading group. This small group setting allows beginning readers to work with a fluent adult model as they make meaning from the text. After children develop fluency with the text and content, the book can be read independently. Children and adults alike will find these books supportive, engaging, and fun!

Nota para los maestros y los padres

¡Leer es una aventura tan emocionante para los niños pequeños! A esta edad están comenzando a integrar su manejo del lenguaje oral con el lenguaje escrito. Para animar a los niños en el camino de la lectura incipiente, los libros deben ser coloridos, estimulantes e interesantes; deben invitar a los jóvenes lectores a explorar la letra impresa y las ilustraciones.

Uso las matemáticas es una nueva colección diseñada para que los niños lean textos sobre el uso de las matemáticas en su vida diaria. En cada libro, los jóvenes lectores explorarán una actividad diferente y resolverán problemas de matemáticas. Cada libro está especialmente diseñado para ayudar a los jóvenes lectores en el proceso de lectura. Los temas familiares llaman la atención de los niños y los invitan a leer y releer una y otra vez. Las fotografías a todo color y el tamaño de la letra ayudan aún más al estudiante en el proceso de lectura.

Además de servir como maravillosos libros ilustrados en escuelas, bibliotecas, hogares y otros lugares donde los niños aprenden a amar la lectura, estos libros han sido especialmente concebidos para ser leídos en un grupo de lectura guiada. Este contexto permite que los lectores incipientes trabajen con un adulto que domina la lectura mientras van determinando el significado del texto. Una vez que los niños dominan el texto y el contenido, el libro puede ser leído de manera independiente. ¡Estos libros les resultarán útiles, estimulantes y divertidos a niños y a adultos por igual!

— Susan Nations, M.Ed., author, literacy coach,
and consultant in literacy development

Today, I am going to the doctor for a checkup. There are many people in the waiting room.

Hoy voy al médico para una revisión. En la sala de espera hay mucha gente.

How many people are in the waiting room?

¿Cuántas personas hay en la sala de espera?

Our appointment is at 1:00. Mom reads a book to me while we wait.

Nuestra cita es a las 1:00. Mientras esperamos, mamá me lee un libro.

What time is it now? How long do I have to wait?

¿Qué hora es ahora? ¿Cuánto tiempo tendré que esperar?

It is our turn! The nurse measures my height. She says I am getting tall!

¡Ya es nuestro turno! La enfermera mide mi altura. ¡Dice que estoy creciendo mucho!

How tall am I?
¿Cuánto mido?

8

Mom says there are twelve inches
in a foot.

- - - - - - - - - - - - - - - - -

Mamá me dice que hay doce pulgadas
en un pie.

How many inches are there in two feet?

¿Cuántas pulgadas hay en dos pies?

11

Next, the nurse asks me to stand on a scale. The scale shows how many pounds I weigh.

Después, la enfermera me pide que me suba a una báscula. La báscula muestra cuántas libras peso.

How much do I weigh?

¿Cuánto peso?

The nurse shows me my chart. I weigh four pounds more than I did last year.

La enfermera me enseña la tabla con mis datos. Peso cuatro libras más que el año pasado.

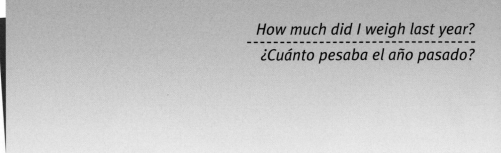

How much did I weigh last year?

¿Cuánto pesaba el año pasado?

14

15

The doctor takes my temperature.
He also looks in my eyes, ears, and mouth.

————————————————

El médico me toma la temperatura.
También me revisa los ojos, los oídos
y la boca.

How many instruments is the doctor
using to check on me?

¿Cuántos instrumentos está usando el médico
para hacerme la revisión?

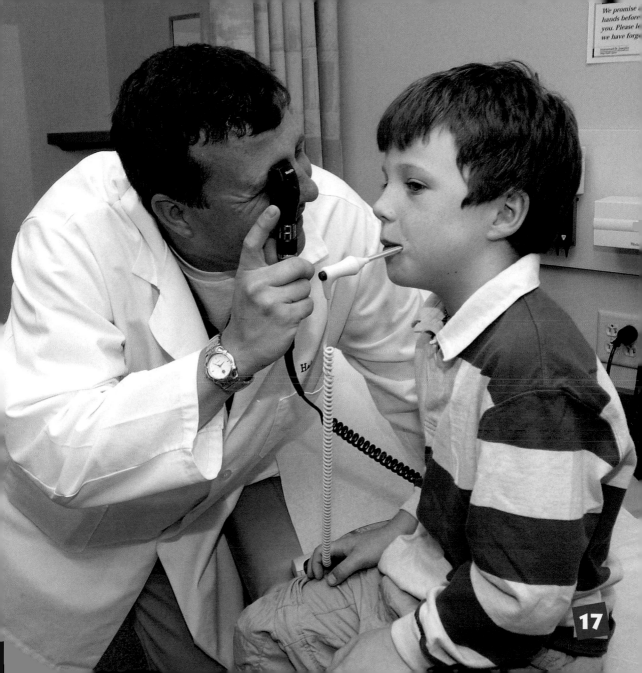

We promise
hands before
you. Please le
we have forge

17

The doctor listens to my heart with a stethoscope. Then, I listen, too. My heart beats once every second.

El médico escucha mi corazón con un estetoscopio. Después, yo escucho también. El corazón me late una vez por segundo.

There are sixty seconds in one minute.
How many times does my heart beat in one minute?

En un minuto hay sesenta segundos.
¿Cuántas veces me late el corazón en un minuto?

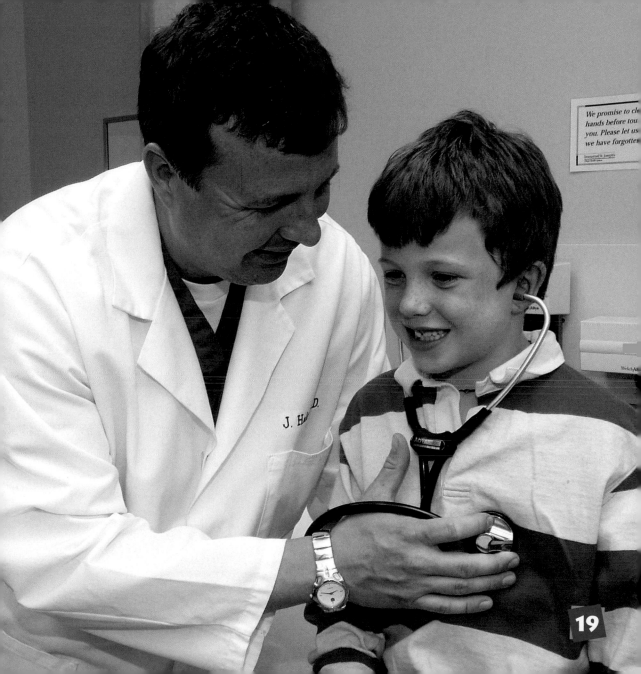

We promise to cle
hands before tou
you. Please let us
we have forgotten

19

My checkup is done! I am healthy. The doctor lets me pick a sticker. I pick the blue one. I like going to the doctor's!

¡Se acabó la revisión! Estoy saludable. El médico me deja elegir una calcomanía. Yo elijo la azul. ¡Me gusta ir al médico!

Which number sticker do I pick?
Hint: Start counting at the top of the stickers.

¿Qué número de calcomanía elijo?
Sugerencia: Empieza a contar desde arriba.

Glossary

appointment — a time to meet someone

checkup — an exam by a doctor to make sure you are not sick

height — how tall you are

instruments — tools to find something out

stethoscope — an instrument used to listen to your heartbeat

temperature — a measurement used to see if you have a fever

weigh — how heavy someone is

Glosario

altura — cuánto mides de los pies a la cabeza

cita — acuerdo entre personas para verse

estetoscopio — instrumento que se usa para escuchar los latidos del corazón

instrumentos — objetos que ayudan a averiguar algo

pesar — determinar cuánto pesa una persona

revisión — examen que realiza un médico para asegurarse de que estás bien de salud

temperatura — medida del calor del cuerpo, que se usa para determinar si tienes fiebre

Answers

Page 4 – 8
Page 6 – 12:30, one-half hour
Page 8 – 49 inches
Page 10 – 24
Page 12 – 59 pounds
Page 14 – 55 pounds
Page 16 – 2
Page 18 – 60 times
Page 20 – 3

Respuestas

Página 4 – 8
Página 6 – la 12:30, media hora
Página 8 – 49 pulgadas
Página 10 – 24
Página 12 – 59 libras
Página 14 – 55 libras
Página 16 – 2
Página 18 – 60 veces
Página 20 – el 3

For More Information/Más información

Books

Counting: Follow That Fish! Math Monsters (series).
  John Burnstein (Weekly Reader® Early
  Learning Library)
How Tall, How Short, How Far Away. David Adler
  (Holiday House)

Libros

Doctor/El médico. People in My Community (series).
  Jacqueline Laks Gorman (Weekly Reader® Early
  Learning Library)
Voy al médico/Going to the Doctor. La primera vez/First
  Time (series). Melinda Beth Radabaugh (Heinemann)

Web sites

Math Baseball
www.funbrain.com/math
Answer math problems to score runs in this online
baseball learning game.

Index

appointment 6
checkup 4, 20
doctor 4, 16, 18, 20
height 8
instruments 16
Mom 6, 10
nurse 8, 12, 14
stethoscope 18
stickers 20
temperature 16
waiting room 4
weighing 12, 14

Índice

altura 8
calcomanías 20
cita 6
enfermera 8, 12, 14
estetoscopio 18
instrumentos 16
mamá 6, 10
médico 4, 16, 18, 20
pesar 12, 14
revisión 4, 20
sala de espera 4
temperatura 16

About the Author

Joanne Mattern is the author of more than 130 books for children. Her favorite subjects are animals, history, sports, and biography. Joanne lives in New York State with her husband, three young daughters, and three crazy cats.

Información sobre la autora

Joanne Mattern ha escrito más de 130 libros para niños. Sus temas favoritos son los animales, la historia, los deportes y las biografías. Joanne vive en el estado de Nueva York con su esposo, sus tres hijas pequeñas y tres gatos juguetones.